the artist's eye

DONA Z. MEILACH

HENRY REGNERY COMPANY • CHICAGO

other books by Dona Z. Meilach

Contemporary Art with Wood
Contemporary Leather
Contemporary Stone Sculpture
Creating Art from Fibers & Fabrics
Creating Art from Anything
Creating with Plaster
Creative Carving
Macramé Accessories
Macramé: Creative Design in Knotting
Making Contemporary Rugs and Wall Hangings
Papercraft
Papier Mâché
Printmaking
Collage and Found Art
  with Elvie Ten Hoor
Creative Stitchery
  with Lee Erlin Snow
Direct Metal Sculpture
  with Donald Seiden
Accent on Crafts
First Book of Bible Heroes (2 volumes)

For Dieter Kober

All photos by Dona and Mel Meilach unless otherwise
    credited.

Published by Henry Regnery Company, 114 West Illinois
    Street, Chicago, Illinois 60610
Manufactured in the United States of America
Library of Congress Catalog Card Number: 79-183817

Acknowledgments

I wish to thank the museums, galleries, and artists that permitted me to use examples from their collections in this book. Special thanks go to Mr. Sam Carini, of the Art Institute of Chicago, for his help in selecting photos.

I am indebted to the art teachers and students who read the manuscript and especially to Mr. Deeks Carroll, M.F.A., of A.A. Stagg High School, Palos Hills, Illinois, for his comments.

I am grateful also to my husband, Dr. Melvin M. Meilach, whose photographic expertise and artistic eye resulted in the scenic and detailed photographs that help to illustrate how the artist sees.

Dona Z. Meilach

Preface

An artist learns to react to the events and objects of the world in a unique way. He sharpens his abilities to observe and transfers his observations into works of art. The aim of this book is to help you understand how the artist translates sensory perceptions into art and how, in turn, his art introduces you to his way of seeing the world. The intention here is to make you more aware of the wealth of sensations all around you, to stimulate you to think and see beyond the visual examples shown, and to expand your awareness of your own environment. By learning to observe line, texture, form, shape, and color of a tree, a road, a shoe, sand, water, sky, and space, to mention only a few elements of our environment, you can become alert to a world that many people miss in a lifetime.

Whether you wish to become an artist or not, learning to see as the artist does will help you to appreciate not only the visual fine arts but other art forms such as music, dance, and drama, plus the effort involved in designing furniture, billboards, posters, clothing, and other commercial art forms.

For a number of years I have used the teaching method presented in this book. I have watched my students become aware of things they had never noticed before and consequently take a greater interest in the fine arts in general. Although this book is designed to complement the elementary, junior high, and high school art curricula, it is a general art education book for anyone wanting to sharpen his or her visual awareness.

Contents

1

Looking at the World

When you view a painting in a museum or at an art gallery, it may look as if the work was done easily, that the artist simply drew his lines, added his paint, and ended up with a painting. But if you've ever tried to capture a scene on paper, you can understand that there are several important decisions you must make before you begin: What to capture? What material to use? (Pencil, ink, chalk, water colors, oils, or a combination?) Where to place the shapes on the paper? What part of the scene should be in what part of the paper? What colors to use? There is also the decision of how to relate one object to another. And, finally, you must decide how to convey the idea or mood you wish to portray.

An artist works with ideas and the objects he sees about him. He transfers mental and visual images to paper, models them in clay, or carves them in stone. How does he capture the things he sees? How does he portray and organize them so that the viewer sees them as he does? For example, how does he take a landscape view, which exists in real space, and capture it on a flat piece of paper so that it has more visual organization than the real scene?

SELF-PORTRAIT.
Fantin La Tour. Oil.
Courtesy: The Art Institute of Chicago

6

These are questions an artist learns to answer both consciously and subconsciously. To an artist a blank piece of paper represents space to be filled with shapes, just as the world is a giant space that is filled with objects of many shapes. The artist must select the shapes he wants to use; his primary concern is relating these objects to space. He distills what he observes in the world and captures it as a new image. At the same time he interprets what he sees in his individual, unique manner and style.

A photograph of moon craters may be interpreted in many ways by individual artists.
Courtesy: Mount Wilson and Palomar Observatories

Henry Stahmer used the shapes of the moon's craters to create a colorful stitchery. The artist does not necessarily try to copy what he sees; rather he uses the images that are around him to spark ideas for designs.

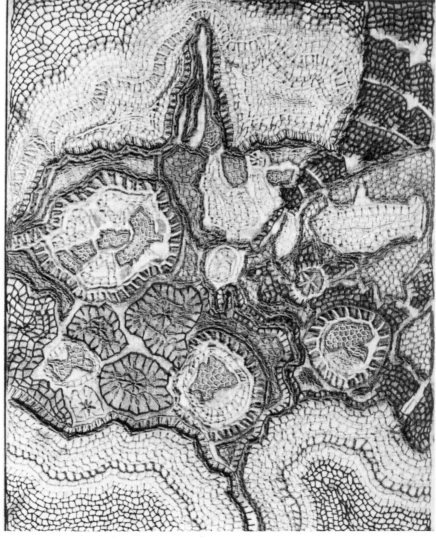

ANTIPODES. Ibram Lassaw.
1960. Bronze, silver, steel.
*Collection: Mrs. Ibram
Lassaw*

The shapes of Ibram Lassaw's
sculpture could have been
inspired by the form of a tree
silhouetted against the sky.

No matter what his ideas, style, or material, an artist's designs include elements other than shape and space. Basically, the other elements are line, form, color, texture, pattern, and subject. Whether you prefer looking at works of art or creating them yourself, learning how the artist views and uses elements of art will make you more keenly aware of the creative process and of how the artist captures his world.

THE VASE OF TULIPS. Paul Cézanne. 1890-1894. Oil on canvas. When Cézanne painted this picture, in the early 1890s, he changed the real appearance of the objects for the sake of the composition of the picture. The flowers are sketchy renderings rather than detailed representations of leaves and petals. The tabletop is tilted at an unreal angle.
Courtesy: The Art Institute of Chicago

GIRAFFE. Ralph Bormacher. 1968. Molten metal dripped over a form captures the essence and shape of the running giraffe.

BULLFIGHT. Edouard Manet.
1865. Oil. Broad brush
strokes and vibrant colors
contribute to Manet's
interpretation of the bullfight
as a festive event.
*Courtesy: The Art Institute
of Chicago*

2

Selecting Materials

It is so easy to overlook the obvious. We see a painting, drawing, sculpture, or other work of art and take its existence for granted. We forget that once the idea evolved in the artist's mind, he had several decisions to make. What material should he use to develop that idea? Would it be better sketched with charcoal, drawn with inks, or brushed with oil paints? Or should he translate his idea as sculpture?

The medium, or material, the artist selects to use for a particular work is based on several factors — availability, the artist's preference for working with certain materials rather than others, and the intended use of the finished piece.

The development of art has been dependent to a large degree on the materials available at any particular time in history. About fifteen thousand years ago, when prehistoric men decorated cave walls, they probably cut designs into the walls with sharp stones; then they applied wet, colored clay to the incised lines with their fingers or with crude brushes. Early art forms existing today reveal shapes carved on shells and antlers and human and animal figures of molded clay.

Egyptian artists carved images in stone; many of these works are so permanent that they can still be seen today in museums throughout the world. Small pieces of colored glass arranged in beautiful designs appeared on the walls and floors of early Christian churches. The glass squares, called tesserae, are the same as those used in mosaic murals, which are still popular today. Paper, which we usually take for granted, was not invented until 105 A.D., when a Chinese government minister looking for a writing surface that would be better than silk and bamboo discovered that the bark of a mulberry tree could be broken into fibers, pounded, and matted into a sheet. For centuries all paper was made from such fibers as rags, hemp, and old fish nets. It was not until the 1880s that paper began to be made from wood pulp.

YOUNG GIRL AT THE HALF OPEN DOOR.
Rembrandt van Rijn. 1645.
Oil paints on canvas permitted the artist to achieve subtle transitions from one tone to another. Rembrandt and other Dutch artists portrayed domestic scenes, landscapes, and everyday people in ordinary situations. This presented a striking contrast to earlier works, in which the subjects were predominantly religious figures, or works commissioned by high ranking officials of the country.
Courtesy: The Art Institute of Chicago

Selecting Materials

It's hard to believe that oil paints, so commonly used today, were developed about five hundred years ago (during the Renaissance, when the arts flourished). Up until that time artists used other materials such as tempera and fresco. Consequently, five hundred years ago wall painting was the storybook technique of the time. It is remarkable how artists from the thirteenth century to the fifteenth century had to work to paint Bible story scenes on the interior walls of churches. First an artist made a huge sketch, called a *sinopie*, on the rough plaster wall or ceiling of the church. He then applied a smooth coat of wet plaster only to the section of the wall that he could paint in one day. His paints, made from colored stones ground into a fine powder and mixed with water, were applied to the wet plaster on the wall. As the plaster hardened, the pigment became part of the wall surface. The result is called a *fresco*, which is the Italian word meaning *fresh*, and it refers to painting on fresh plaster. The entire ceiling and walls of the Sistine Chapel, much of it done by Michelangelo, were painted by this fresco method.

THE DELPHIC SIBYL. Michelangelo. 15th century. Fresco. Adding colored water-soluble pigment to wet plaster was a slow, demanding, tedious process. Michelangelo spent six years completing one of the most astonishing accomplishments in the history of art—the fresco on the ceiling of the Sistine Chapel, which portrays scenes from the Old Testament and images of mythological beings. Although architectural settings of the fresco seem to be made of stone, the entire work is actually painted on a flat surface. *Courtesy: Alinari, Florence, Italy*

DANCERS IN THE WINGS. Edgar Degas. 1890. Pastels on paper. Pastels are a colored chalk-like crayon used for drawing on paper. Degas liked pastels because he could use them to create the illusion of soft, sheer fabrics. *Courtesy: The Art Institute of Chicago*

DELPHICA

Another popular material of the Renaissance was *tempera*, which was made by mixing ground powdered pigment with egg yolk, a protein solvent. Temperas were applied with a brush to wood panels that were first coated with gesso, also a form of dilute wet plaster. The gesso coat provided a hard, smooth surface and prevented the wood from absorbing the paint. The temperas that artists use today are made with a protein other than egg yolk, but the properties remain the same: they are fast drying, easy to use, and fine detail may be achieved with temperas by using tiny brushes. Andrew Wyeth, an American artist whose works are popular today, often prefers temperas to oils for his detailed, realistic paintings.

YOUNG AMERICA. Andrew Wyeth. 1950. Tempera. Wyeth is able tc achieve fine line and detail with tempera.
Courtesy: Pennsylvania Academy of Fine Arts

THE THREE CROSSES.
Rembrandt van Rijn. 1653.
Etching. Dry point is a
printmaking process. In this
process the drawing is etched
into a copper plate, and the
plate is inked. The paper
then is pressed against and
into the inked lines of the
plate to produce a print.
*Courtesy: The Art Institute
of Chicago*

17

The practice of mixing pigments with oils is credited to the early fifteenth-century Flemish painter Jan van Eyck (1370-1440). Perhaps van Eyck was tempted to mix pigment with oils rather than egg yolk because in the cold climate of the Netherlands temperas tended to dry too quickly and, sometimes, to freeze. Oils dry slowly, allowing the artist time to work one color into and over another and to achieve subtle transition of tones. Van Eyck and later fifteenth century Italian painters, such as Raphael and da Vinci, applied oil paint to wood panels as they had the temperas.

But it was in early sixteenth-century Venice that oil painting developed most rapidly. Walls and ceilings of new palaces and public places were to be decorated with battle scenes and mythological and historical subjects. In addition, churches were to be decorated with depictions of religious subjects. Oils worked on canvas were much easier to handle than frescoes; the range of colors was greater, and the artist could work at an easel and then attach the canvas to the wall or ceiling.

DAVID. Donatello. 15th century. Bronze casting. *Courtesy: Uffizi Gallery, Florence, Italy*

PLANT FORM. Leah Balsham. 1967. Ceramic objects are created when moist clay is formed, dried, and fired in a kiln at temperatures over 1000° F. Special coloring, called glazes, may be painted onto the dried clay surface before it is fired. *Courtesy: The Art Institute of Chicago*

RHINOCEROS. Ann Arnold.
1964. With assembled and
carved pine wood the artist
is able to catch the gesture
and shape of the animal
without being realistic.
*Courtesy: Fishbach Gallery,
New York*

THE OUTSIDE OF A SOLDIER.
Edward Higgins. 1958.
Welded steel and plaster
assembled.
*Courtesy: The Museum of
Modern Art, New York*

Acrylics, a recent addition to the artist's paint box, are a combination of synthetic materials that are permanent, fast drying, more brilliant in color than oils and temperas, and relatively easy to use.

When the printing press was invented (by Johann Gutenberg in the mid-fifteenth century), the practice of making multiple prints from one plate evolved. *Printmaking* methods involve carving a design into a wood, metal, or linoleum block; inking it; and pressing it on different pieces of paper to make more than one finished work, or print, from one block, or plate.

New media continued to evolve, through the centuries, as artists sought additional ways to work. The idea of pasting objects to the surface of a painting began in the early 1900s when Georges Braque and Pablo Picasso incorporated pieces of paper on their oil paintings. From this grew the medium of *collage*, derived from the French word *coller* meaning *to paste*.

COLLAGE. Ann Ryan. 1953. Fabrics pasted in a composition are called a "collage," from the French word "coller," meaning "to paste."
Courtesy: The Museum of Modern Art, New York

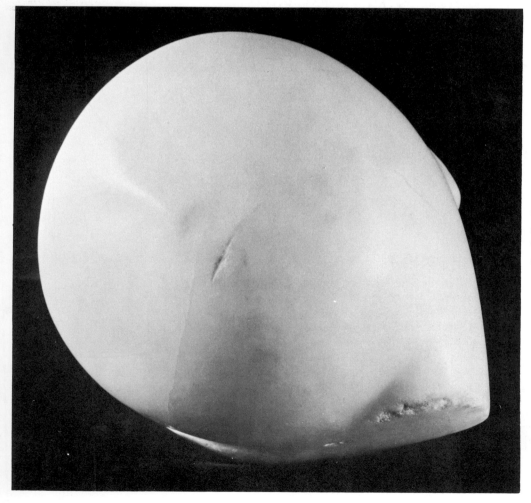

PROMETHEUS. Constantin Brancusi. 1911. Marble.
Courtesy: The Philadelphia Museum of Art

FISH. Laszlo Moholy-Nagy.
1940. Plastic.
*Courtesy: The Art Institute
of Chicago*

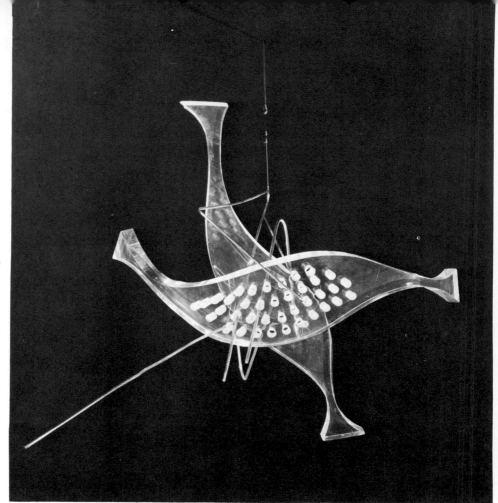

MANAO TUPAPAU
(Watched by the Spirits of
the Dead). Paul Gauguin. 1895.
Woodcut print colored with
stencils.
*Courtesy: The Art Institute
of Chicago*

Selecting Materials

For centuries sculptors had been accustomed to working with cast metals. In the early 1930s they began to borrow ideas from industry and created welded metal sculptures using an oxyacetylene torch. Also about this time stone and wood, always popular for carving, began to appear as *assembled* works. Due to modern chemical developments of strong, permanent, weather-resistant cements, stone and wood could be used easily in assembled works. In the twentieth century all kinds of plastics also began to be used in sculptural forms.

In the works illustrated throughout this book try to identify the techniques and materials used. You will notice that fabric is used for collage and weaving, clay for pottery and sculpture, stone and wood for carving, and metal for casting. In many instances artists combine media and techniques for additional variety.

WOVEN AND KNOTTED RUG. Frieda Imling Fodor. 1965.

3

Using Line

If you place a pencil in your hand and a piece of paper in front of you, you will quite automatically begin to doodle, to write your name, or to draw something — anything. You are unconsciously using one of the most important elements of art — *line*.

Look at the lines you have made. Observe that they vary in size, shape, and direction. Their appearance also will vary, depending on the instrument you used: a hard or soft pencil, chalk, a pen, or a brush. The character of the line will depend on the material you used: pencil lead, ink, paint. All of these materials produce distinct lines. The skill, personality, and mood of the person drawing also determines the appearance of a line. If you write your name when you are rushed or tense, the lines will suggest your feeling. But if you write slowly when you are in a dreamy mood, the lines will have a different character.

Objects do not have lines around their outer edges, yet when we draw an object on paper, we think of its outer edge as line. The petals of a daisy are not edged in black, but when we draw a daisy, we may begin with its outline. In looking at the accompanying examples, think about whether or not the objects really have black lines around them. As you observe people, buildings, and objects, think of the lines you would need if you had to draw them. When you see these same objects in paintings, ask yourself how the artist used line to develop his picture.

As you learn to *look* at lines, you will observe that they are either straight or curved or a combination of the two. Draw several freehand lines that are both straight and curved; make them move, wiggle, curl, and bend but observe that they are always basically straight or curved.

Using Line

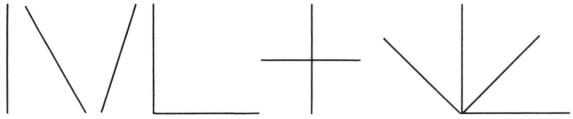

What other characteristics of line can you observe? Lines have *direction*. They are horizontal, vertical, diagonal, or a series of curves. They also may join and cross one another.

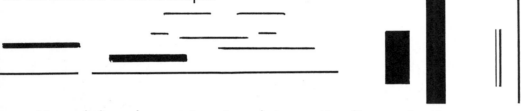

Of course, lines vary in length and width; therefore, they have size. They are long and short, broad and thin. Such lines also may be considered to have shape.

Lines *define* shapes. A series of connecting lines going in different directions and enclosing space creates squares, circles, hexagons, ovals, and other shapes.

Enclosed lines form recognizable objects. But do lines really exist around these objects?

THE DRINKERS.
Vincent Van Gogh.
Thick and thin curving,
jagged, and broken lines
suggest tension, movement,
and haste.
*Courtesy: The Art Institute
of Chicago*

What kinds of lines would
you have to use if you were
to draw this landscape?
An artist knows that linear
patterns exist in nature, and
he may use nature as his
source of inspiration for
creating a work of art.

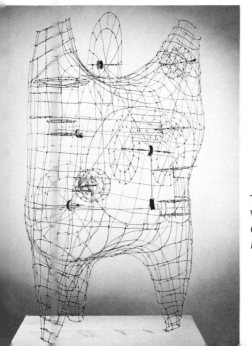

TORSO. Harry Kramer. 1964.
Wire construction.
*Courtesy: Tate Gallery,
London*

Using Line

The artist is conscious of how he uses line and the effect of the tool and the medium he uses. He also exploits other characteristics: a line can be heavy, light, bold, jabbing, broken, curved, angular, flowing, jagged, tight, loose, distinct, flexible, smooth, rough, or sketchy.

Linear patterns are obvious in manmade objects. Lines wide apart at the bottom and coming together at the top give a work perspective. Horizontal lines that appear narrower and shorter at the top of the picture also suggest distance.

The artist sees the directions and linear design radiating in a sliced piece of fruit . . .

. . . and interprets it in a work of art. Detail from a stitched wall hanging by John Smith.
Courtesy: Humble Oil and Refining Co., Houston, Texas

There are lines in the wings of a butterfly . . .

. . . in a fence, and in the riggings of industry.

Using Line

Line is used also to express *emotion*, *idea*, and *space*. Horizontal lines such as those that may dominate a landscape painting suggest quiet and rest. A series of diagonal lines may create a feeling of unrest. A group of squiggles may be comical. Vertical lines make an object appear to soar skyward, which is one reason that most churches are built with an emphasis on vertical lines.

PORTRAIT OF GUSTAVE SCHIEFLER. Ernest Kirchner. 1922. Pen and ink drawing. *Courtesy: The Art Institute of Chicago*

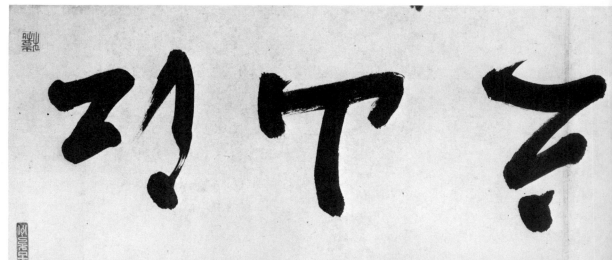

SCENE OF THE PASSION.
Georges Rouault. 1938. Oil.
Thick and thin lines are
painted in many directions
and shapes.
*Courtesy: The Art Institute
of Chicago*

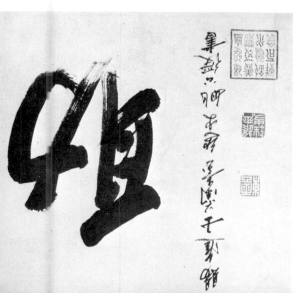

CALLIGRAPHY.
Characteristics of line are
illustrated in these ink-
brushed Oriental letters.

Lines that begin far apart at the bottom of the paper and move closer together toward the top give the illusion of receding distance, or *perspective*. Combinations of lines can suggest rapid or slow motion. Even the movement and direction of your eyebrows, considered as lines, can suggest your reaction to an incident or an idea; it is this eyebrow line that cartoonists often exploit when they indicate the mood of their characters.

In the accompanying pictures observe the characteristics of the lines and how you react to them.

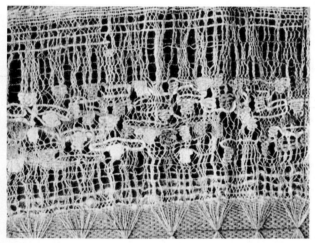

DETAIL OF IKAT WEAVING. Karen Chang. Threads woven alternately loose and tight have characteristics similar to drawn lines.

LINEAR CONSTRUCTION NO. 4 in BLACK AND GRAY. Naum Gabo. 1953. Aluminum and stainless steel. *Courtesy: The Art Institute of Chicago, gift of Suzette Morton Zurcher*

UNTITLED. Harry Bertoia.
1964. Welded brass and
copper rods.
*Courtesy: Staempfli Gallery,
New York, collection of
Mr. Peter Gimpel, London*

GABLES IN LUNEBERG,
NO. 2404. Lyonel Feininger.
1924. Woodcut. Lines are
used in many directions,
thicknesses, and shapes.
*Courtesy: The Art Institute
of Chicago*

Working with Shapes

For centuries artists worked with shapes they had observed and painted these shapes in a realistic, recognizable manner. Their shapes suggested real *volume* and had *mass* and *contour*. It was the artist Paul Cézanne, in the late 1800s, who stated that every natural shape could be reduced to one of the following simple geometric shapes: "the cylinder, the sphere, and the cone." In Cézanne's paintings of landscapes, people, and still life, shapes are easily recognizable, but they are not executed as precisely as the real objects. He believed that in painting, objects had to be put in proper perspective so that each side of an object, or plane, is directed toward a central point. Artists who followed Cézanne were so intrigued by his theory that they continued to reshape and place what they saw in new, not necessarily realistic relationships. Consequently, artists began to observe things in a new way.

YELLOW NO. 9.
Fernand Léger. Hand woven wool tapestry. Geometric shapes in an abstract composition.
Courtesy: Charles E. Slatkin Galleries, New York

THE GULF OF MARSEILLES SCENE FROM L'ESTAQUE. Paul Cézanne. Houses, chimneys, and mountains may be viewed as inter-related cones, cylinders, spheres, and rectangles.
Courtesy: The Metropolitan Museum of Art, New York

FIGURE IV. 1960.
Hans Aeschbacher. 1960.
A stone sculpture created
from cubes is designed to
confine rectangular cubic
spaces between some of the
shapes.
Courtesy: Artist

Shapes are found everywhere
—in the pebbles themselves
and in the light and shade
that fall upon them.

It was Cézanne's theory of presenting natural shapes as geometric solids that evolved into the art movement called Cubism, which developed in the early twentieth century. Using Cézanne's lesson of seeing natural shapes as geometric solids, Cubist painters Pablo Picasso, Georges Braque, and Juan Gris worked almost exclusively with geometric shapes in a picture plane to evolve a whole new world of artistic vision.

A display of glass bottles illustrates uses of man-made shape in a decorative manner. Ovals, cylinders, circles, and curves interrelate.

VILLAGE STREET. Lyonel Feininger. 1929. In this work geometric abstract shapes still suggest realism. Clues to the meaning of a work sometimes appear in the title. But realism and recognition of objects are not always important. The interrelation of shapes in a balanced, harmonious composition is the aim of the artist.
Courtesy: The Art Institute of Chicago

Manmade objects are created by means of shapes that repeat and relate. Circular shapes are repeated in the spokes, the axles, the hub, and the screws.

But most artists, whether they paint realistically or in an accentuated geometric manner, continue to take their inspiration from nature and man-made forms. Cézanne's paintings have their beginnings in objects that he arranged and rearranged according to his theory of presenting natural shapes as geometric solids, thereby freeing the artist from painting as if he were a camera trying to recreate a scene in every minute detail. Cézanne's theory carried over into other art media such as sculpture, ceramics, and architecture and directed the course of art along a new path.

THE BACK. Henri Matisse. 1909. Bronze. Three portrayals.
Courtesy: The Museum of Modern Art, New York

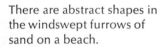
There are abstract shapes in the windswept furrows of sand on a beach.

About 1914.

About 1929.

Henri Matisse's studies of the figure at different periods of his career illustrate the artist's progression from an almost realistic portrayal of the human figure to a more abstract composition based on geometric forms. In the 1909 composition the form has movement and curves; the surfaces are rounded in a naturalistic manner. By 1914 Matisse extracted the essence of the figure and simplified the shapes considerably, retaining the gesture and feeling of the position of the figure. In the 1929 version the torso is further simplified into huge cylindrical shapes.

After the Cubists initiated the use of known geometric shapes, other artists began to elongate and distort these shapes; the result was the beginning of abstract art. Abstract art took several directions. First, think of abstract art as using shapes that do not necessarily represent recognizable objects. A shape may have evolved from an object, but the artist was not interested in portraying the object realistically; instead, he changed it to portray an idea or feeling about the object. Instead of painting a realistic picture of an elephant the artist may be able to convey the strength and mass of the animal by employing the elements of color, texture, and line in such a way as to give you the feeling of elephant without giving you an exact replica.

JACQUES LIPCHITZ AND HIS WIFE. Amedeo Modigliani. 1916. *Courtesy: The Art Institute of Chicago*

ST. GEORGE AND THE BEGGAR. El Greco. About 1600. Oil. Distorted shapes that appear longer than they would be in reality were used by the Spanish painter El Greco. His figures appear extremely important, and they stand out in a field of endless space and sky. *Courtesy: The Art Institute of Chicago*

LIPCHITZ *modigliani*

41

Second, abstract art grew to a point in which geometric shapes completely dissolved into a movement of line, color, texture, and pattern so that it was completely informal, sometimes haphazard, yet aesthetically pleasing. To enjoy abstract art you do not have to find an answer to the often-posed question: What is it? What a work represents in content is not always important. What matters is that you feel a kinship with the work, that, due to the arrangement of the art elements, it expresses the artist's feeling so vividly that you react to it in an emotional manner.

STONE HEAD. Amedeo Modigliani. About 1912. In his paintings and sculptures Modigliani elongated the ovals and cylinders in his figures. He was greatly influenced by simplified forms found in sculptures from primitive African tribes. *Courtesy: The Philadelphia Museum of Art*

5

Understanding Form

Once you are aware of shapes as the artist sees them, it is only another short step along the art appreciation path to learn to see *form* as the artist does. Not every artist will agree on what form is or even be able to define it; yet each artist ably captures form on paper and in scores of other art media: stone, clay, fibers, and many more. What is form? Webster describes it as, *the shape and structure of anything: figure.* For example, your figure is a form determined by its shape and its skeleton.

A child who draws two stick lines for a person's arms has innocently captured the essence of the arms' structure, which helps to determine the shape of the arms, whether they are long or short. If the child then drew two ovals over those stick lines, he would give the arm another dimension — fat or thin. The combined drawings — one giving length, the other, thickness — would determine the actual form of the arm. The artist who wishes to draw an arm with a feeling of reality understands both inner structure and shape, which result in form.

You can readily recognize the form of an automobile. You appreciate that the steel understructure and its shape help to determine the overall form. You would say spontaneously that an orange has a round form. If you analyze what is within an orange, you can see that inner structure and shape determine the object we recognize as an orange.

The artist learns to analyze an object's form. To draw a tree he might draw the branches first and let their structure and shape determine the tree's form. Try this yourself by collecting examples of leaves from several kinds of trees and drawing the veins, which are the skeletal structure of a leaf. Then draw the shape of the leaf by using a boundary line that connects the ends of the veins. A maple leaf would have veins and a resulting shape different from that of an elm or oak leaf, yet all are leaf forms.

Modern artists often are so intrigued by the structure and function of form that they use parts of a form as the entire subject of a work. One artist, captivated by the movement and shape of the joints in the elbow, created a metal sculpture derived from an understanding of that form.

To create sculpture and architecture you must have a knowledge of form. Perhaps you have tried to create an animal over a wire armature. If you want to make a giraffe, the wire is bent and shaped to result in a form different from that of a dog.

Form alone does not equal art. It must be combined with aesthetic virtues. A skeleton of an animal and its shape in a museum exhibit are simple, natural, factual presentations of form. An artist may use that presentation as a point of departure to create a work of art that is individually expressive. By selecting a material such as paint or stone the artist can present a form in a variety of real and abstract images that may be more exciting and aesthetically appealing than the original form.

RECLINING FIGURE. Henry Moore. 1945-1946. Elm wood. The artist has utilized his knowledge of form to suggest an inner structure, around which he has developed simple abstract shapes that give the feeling of a reclining figure.
Courtesy: Henry Moore, photo, Errol Jackson, collection, Cranbrook Academy of Arts, Michigan

The skeletal structure
of a building
determines its form.
*Photographed at
Mount Mary College,
Milwaukee, Wisconsin*

Have you ever heard anyone refer to an artist's work as *free form*? This term means that an artist has created an object that has no real internal organization; its shape alone is its form, but it still has mass, volume, and contour. A rock or stone is an example of a free-form object. The artist, deriving his inspiration for a painting from the rock, may abstract the rock's form in any way he likes because he has no internal structure to confine him. He depicts the rock's contour and suggests its weight. And in the final stage his work may not suggest any recognizable form at all but may be beautiful by virtue of the way the artist has developed the form using the elements of art.

Veins make up the structure that determines a leaf's form. Print made from leaves by LaVeda Hinkson.

To create an animal over an armature you must understand that its skeletal structure determines its form.

6

Organizing Work in Space

We live in space. We intuitively organize objects in space when we arrange furniture in a room, place pictures on a wall, or set dishes on a table. Artists are acutely conscious of space and how to arrange objects in it. A canvas is basically a white space that must be filled with painted objects in an interesting manner. The forms of a sculpture must be created so that they exist effectively in space and are harmoniously placed.

To begin this discussion of space we must understand the difference between space requirements for a painting and those for a sculpture. A painting has only height and width and, therefore, exists only in these two dimensions. Shapes may be drawn so that they appear to have deep spatial perspective, but in reality the surface of a painting is only two dimensional. Painting and all flat surface art work are considered *two-dimensional* art — having the dimensions of height and width.

What makes a work three dimensional? If a work of art has height, width, and depth, it then occupies space in three dimensions. Sculpture and architecture, which occupy space in height, width, and depth, are considered *three-dimensional* art forms. As you exist in space, you occupy three dimensions. A sculpture of you also would be three dimensional. However, if you were drawn on a piece of paper, the portrayal would be two dimensional. Why? Because on paper *only* height and width can exist, although depth can be suggested by shading and perspective.

INTERRUPTED READING. Jean Corot. 1865-1870. Oil. A painting is a two-dimensional work of art because it has height and width. The figure is the positive shape; the area around it is the negative space, which must be designed as carefully as the positive shape. *Courtesy: The Art Institute of Chicago*

CURVED FORMS WITH
STRING. Barbara Hepworth.
The artist consciously breaks
up space with positive forms
made of wood, metal, and
string. Observe how spaces
between the strings are
developed into graduated
sizes and shapes.
*Courtesy: The Detroit
Institute of Arts*

DOG. Alberto Giacometti.
1956. Bronze. A sculpture is
a three-dimensional work of
art: it occupies space in
height, width, and depth.

Through the years artists have taken great liberties with rules of perspective for the sake of distortion and personal ideas they wished to convey. Modern artists often deliberately disregard or alter true perspective. The Cubists (see Juan Gris's painting, page 33) purposely overlapped shapes in flat space. Cézanne neglected perspective when it did not suit his purpose in a particular work, often tilting a tabletop to conform to his principles of volume in space. Some artists will distort perspective to startle us or dramatize an idea.

Perspective as observed in reality is captured in a two-dimensional photograph. An artist develops scenes having perspective in paintings by portraying those objects that appear in the distance smaller than those in the foreground. Using curved and diagonal lines that meet at a diminishing point also helps to achieve perspective in a painting. *Photo: Mel Meilach*

MADONNA AND CHILD.
Hans Memling. 1485. Oil and
tempera on wood panel. In
the fifteenth century, when
artists learned about the
scientific principles of
perspective, they drew
landscapes and mirrors in a
composition to give the
illusion of depth.
*Courtesy: The Art Institute
of Chicago*

RACE TRACK NEAR PARIS.
Edouard Manet. 1864. Oil on
canvas. What elements in the
photograph on page 52 are
similar to those the artist
uses in this painting to
achieve the feeling of near
and far in two dimensions?
*Courtesy: The Art Institute
of Chicago*

Organizing Work in Space

Another principle that artists deal with is *positive* or *negative space*. Positive space refers to the space occupied by the shape of an object. In Corot's painting *Interrupted Reading* (page 49), the positive space is occupied by the figure of the girl. The space around her and between her arm and head are negative spaces. Negative spaces must be designed to be as pleasing as positive shapes so that they satisfy the eye and preserve the picture's balance. Abstract painters frequently are concerned only with the interplay of positive shape and negative space on canvas.

In the accompanying drawing the black rectangular shape exists in open space that is boundless. If we place that shape within a square, it is defined in space and is related to the boundary line. The rectangle becomes a positive shape; the area around it is the negative space. In the first circle the line is positive, and the area within is negative. However, when the circle is solid and placed within a square boundary, the solid shape is positive, and the space around it is negative.

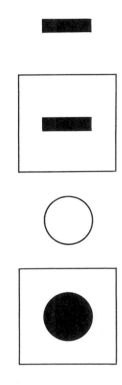

THE BASKET OF APPLES. Paul Cézanne. 1890. Oil on canvas. Cézanne accomplished perspective in this painting in two ways; first, he drew the edge of the table to the back right of the picture on an angle. The table appears to move away from the horizontal edge in the lower part of the painting. Second, Cézanne placed objects behind one another and actually tilted the basket on end. Consequently, we get the feeling that the table and objects exist in deep space even though they are painted on a flat plane. *Courtesy: The Art Institute of Chicago*

SUNDAY AFTERNOON ON THE ISLAND OF LA GRANDE JATTE. Georges Seurat. 1884–1886. Oil on canvas. A wide expanse of space is presented in Seurat's scene, with people and objects having been arranged carefully. Dark and light shapes are set forth so that the eye is carried from side to side and then to the distant background at the top of the painting. This huge painting was made with tiny dots of pure color, replacing the brush strokes with which oils are usually applied. Seurat called his technique "divisionism" because he was trying to show how light divides color.
Courtesy: The Art Institute of Chicago

TAPESTRY. Czechoslovakian. 1968. Woven yarns. When no attention is given to sizes of objects or their placement in deep space, perspective is ignored, and objects appear to be on the same plane standing on top of one another.

55

The sculptor must think of positive and negative space in terms of three dimensions. His forms both *occupy* space and often *enclose* it in a design that is appealing from any angle you may view it. In José de Rivera's chrome steel sculpture on page 44 the steel is the positive shape, and the areas it encloses are the negative spaces. Observe how carefully these negative spaces have been designed so that they interrelate with the sculpture; they constantly change as you walk around the piece.

Another obvious example of the importance of negative space is in Hans Aeschbacher's stone sculpture *Figure IV 1960*, on page 35. As an integral part of the composition the cubes and rectangles purposely have been placed to enclose negative space. As you sharpen your awareness of the way objects exist and interrelate to the space around and within them, you will heighten your ability to see as the artist sees and to appreciate how the artist applies his vision to his art.

SYLVETTE BLEUE VIOLETTE. Pablo Picasso. 1954. Oil. Picasso's unique experiments in painting purposely disregarded perspective. He attempted to show a three-dimensional object, in this case a person, as though all dimensions, or sides, could be seen at the same time from one place. For example, the side of the head is shown next to a front view of the face. *Courtesy: The Art Institute of Chicago*

OVERLAY OF PLOTS. James Warren Felter. 1967. Abstract painters are concerned mainly with the interplay of positive and negative shapes on a surface. They feel free to express themselves in any manner at all. Abstract paintings often appear haphazardly composed, but actually the canvas space has been carefully designed. *Courtesy: Artist*

7

Creating with Color

Color surrounds us. Each of us reacts to color in our own way. Certain colors make us look or feel better. We decorate our homes with color. There is color in the sky, the ocean, in our clothing — in everything around us. So accustomed are we to color that we rarely think of it in scientific terms. Color actually is light reflected from an object. Green is the color of the light reflected to our eyes when we see grass; an apple may reflect as red light. Scientists have explored the nature of white light as it is passed through a spectrum and broken into the colors of a rainbow.

The artist usually approaches the concept of color with more of an emotional rather than a scientific knowledge. He thinks of color as creating a mood: a feeling of gaiety, happiness, excitement, despair, gloom, or sadness. He knows that color can create lines, can suggest and define shapes and space. It can make an object appear light or heavy, transparent or dense.

Color is an important element of art. The artist knows what happens when colors mix. One of his tools is the color wheel, which helps to guide him to the usual and unusual color relationships. The artist begins with what are called *the primary colors*: red, yellow, and blue. When he combines primary colors, he creates *secondary colors*: thus yellow and blue together equal shades of blue-green; blue and red mixed equal violets; red and yellow produce oranges.

THE OLD GUITARIST. Pablo Picasso. 1903. Oil on canvas. Painted entirely in shades of blue, the picture's tone and subject matter are somber.
Courtesy: The Art Institute of Chicago

The artist can achieve additional color combinations by mixing these secondary colors — blue-greens, violets, and oranges — for another range, called *tertiary colors*, which yield soft, muted shades.

Another convenience of the color wheel is that it tells the artist how one color affects another. Those close to each other will harmonize and result in a softer, more serene arrangement of colors than those that contrast. *Contrasting colors*, those opposite each other on the color wheel, will clash and produce a more shocking feeling than those that harmonize. Colors near to each other on the wheel, but not next to each other, such as red and green, are called *complementary colors* and can result in visual excitement when placed together.

White and black are neutral colors. Combining them produces gray. If black is added to a color, it produces a grayed effect. If white is added to a color, you get a softer, paler tone of the original.

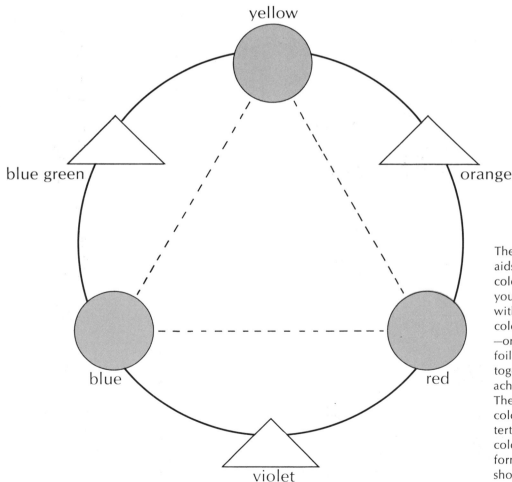

The color wheel is a tool that aids the artist in determining color usage. Try making your own color wheel. Begin with a dab of each primary color—yellow, blue, and red —on a piece of aluminum foil. Mix the primary colors together one at a time to achieve secondary colors. Then mix the secondary colors with one another for tertiary colors. Arrange the colors in such a way that they form a wheel like the one shown here.

THE LION HUNT. Eugene Delacroix. Oil on canvas. A swirling movement is created with various shades of reds to invoke a feeling of high excitement and nervous energy.
Courtesy: The Art Institute of Chicago

READY TO WEAR. Stuart Davis. 1955. Oil.
Courtesy: The Art Institute of Chicago

The artist is concerned also with the amounts of colors he chooses to use. Some artists strive for perfect balance among colors and may elect to use equal amounts of different colors. Others think that for a more exciting canvas one color should be allowed to dominate, with secondary colors being used in lesser amounts. But artists do not necessarily consult a color wheel for their ideas; they can observe and be inspired by pleasing combinations in nature. Blue and violet flowers may have orange centers; a red rose may have tinted yellow leaves.

TWO LITTLE CIRCUS GIRLS.
Pierre Auguste Renoir. 1870.
Courtesy: The Art Institute of Chicago

LA TOILETTE. Mary Cassatt.
*Courtesy: The Art Institute
of Chicago*

BEDROOM AT ARLES.
Vincent Van Gogh. 1888. Oil.
*Courtesy: The Art Institute
of Chicago*

Creating with Color

PORTRAIT OF MAX JACOB.
Jean Metzinger. 1913. Oil on
canvas. Wild colors
developed by the Fauves,
which means "wild beasts,"
are combined with cubist
shapes.
Private collection

FOUR PERSONAGES.
Enrico Baj. 1968. Collage and
oil. Assorted print fabrics,
ribbon metals, and other
materials are combined in
this fantastic portrait, which
shows honors being
bestowed on everyone.
*Collection: Mr. & Mrs.
Donn Shapiro,
Glencoe, Illinois*

ESSEX. John Chamberlain.
1960. Relief sculpture.
Automobile parts and other
metals were welded and
painted with acrylics.
*Courtesy: The Museum of
Modern Art, New York*
*(Gift of Mr. & Mrs. Robert C.
Scull and purchase)*

THE EARTH IS A MAN. Matta.
1942. Oil. Matta's paintings
are highly colorful and
imaginative. They are filled
with mythical demonic
beings on other-worldly
landscapes that have
strange psychic vegetations.
Private collection

PINK BIRD. Morris Graves.
1951. Encaustic. The artist
often painted birds that
have a mystical, symbolic,
spiritual quality—a possible
influence of his studies of
Zen Buddhism in Japan.
Private collection

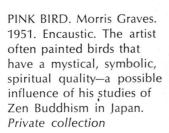

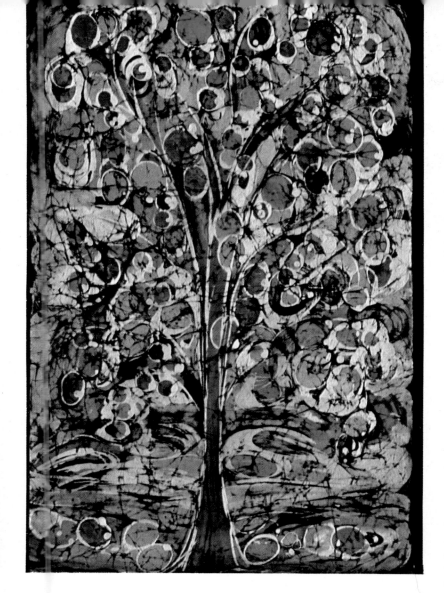

NATURE IN BLOOM.
Blanche Carstenson. 1970.
Batik on textile. The textures
and glories of nature's colors
are captured in a process
that involves dyeing fabric
that has been partly covered
with wax—an ancient
Javanese method for fabric
decorating.
Photo: Dona Meilach

FORM. Roger Kotoske. 1971.
Colored polyester resin.
Plastic, one kind of material
developed for industrial use
and adapted by artists, has
added an exciting new scope
to sculpture.
Courtesy: Artist

HIGH SEAS. Philip Pavia. 1965. Marble. An unusual handling of stone for sculpture in a completely modern, abstract manner. Early stone sculptures usually portrayed human figures, portraits, and animals. *Collection: Leonard Boedel, Williamstown, Massachusetts Courtesy: Martha Jackson Gallery, New York*

STONE GROUP. Mary Bauermeister. 1964. In an assemblage of pebbles the artist uses nature as the material and subject of this work and organizes the pebbles in an artistic arrangement. *Courtesy: Galeria Bonino Ltd., New York*

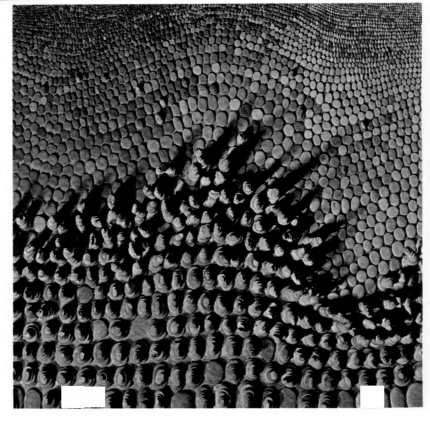

SEA CHANGE—SAND
FOUNTAIN NO. 18. Ann
Wiseman. 1966. Natural
colors of objects such as
sand, wood, rocks, and coral
are combined with metal.
*Courtesy: Chase Manhattan
Bank, New York*

WEAVING. Japanese. Late Edo
Period. Color is important
to every medium, pattern,
and subject.

73

Not all artists use color to reflect their moods. Even when Paul Gauguin was unhappy and ill, he continued to paint in bright colors that reflected the Tahitian scenes that surrounded him. The bright colors that he used give no indication of his misery.

The Impressionist painters were interested in capturing the effect of natural light on colors. To capture this elusive phenomenon of nature's light they painted in short, quick strokes, squeezing the paint directly onto their brushes or palette, and mixed colors only occasionally on the canvas. A series of paintings of the same subject — such as the one done on Notre Dame Cathedral in Paris, by Claude Monet — painted at different times of the day vividly illustrates that objects do change color under different light.

CEREMONIAL SHIELD. Mary Sue Foster. 1970. Shades of brown and beige are considered earth colors. Natural jute and sisal made into rope are used for subtle tonal changes in this macramé hanging.

BIRTH OF A STAR. Thea Tewi. 1968. Stalactite marble has subtle gradations of golden ochres, ranging from a light cream to a brown. *Courtesy: La Boetie Gallery, New York*

RED SPIRAL. Hans Hofmann. 1955. Oil on canvas. *Courtesy: André Emmerich Gallery, New York*

All artists are not the same kind of colorists. Rembrandt's works are generally dark, but they are highlighted with brighter tones of somber colors to show the light that emphasized and dramatized. In Rembrandt's *Young Girl at the Half Open Door*, on page 13, natural light seems to flow in from a side window to illuminate portions of the figure as though urging it out from the shadows.

Some modern painters, such as Hans Hofmann, are pure colorists. For this type of painter the interplay of colors of every kind skittering across the canvas appears to be of greater interest than the subject, shape, or design.

Color is personal, expressive, and altered by light. It is an important element for both artist and viewer.

MONOANGULATED SURFACE IN SPACE. Max Bill. Shiny metal reflects light and changing colors. *Courtesy: The Detroit Institute of Arts*

76

8

Using Texture

The textures in some plants, such as this artichoke, offer a rough, prickly look and feel, as compared to the petals of a rose, which are smooth and soft.

Texture is the surface quality of a material. We think of texture as something we want to touch. The rough texture of packing cardboard is obviously different from the smoother texture of this page of paper. Some textures are so rough that they are unpleasant to touch — such as the outside of a pineapple. Others, such as a kitten's fur, are soft and silky, and we like to rub our hands over them.

We think of texture primarily as something to feel, but it is also a quality we can see. Training oneself to look for textures helps to develop artistic vision. The artist constantly seeks textures that he can translate into his work for visual and tactile excitement.

Notice the differences in textures of the clothes you are wearing. Are your shoes smooth or grainy? How does the texture of nylon hosiery differ from cotton socks? The texture of a woolly sweater feels and looks different from that of a woven straw hat.

Using Texture

The contents of a refrigerator offer a wide variety of textures. Notice the skins of different fruits, the surfaces of cream cheese and butter, the leaves from lettuce or cabbage. Stand among trees and flowers or on a city street and really *see* texture, feel it, think about it. The leaf of a weed may be rough and prickly, while that of a tree may be smooth. Textures vary in bricks, wood, roof tiles, and building stones. As you become aware of texture, you will consciously sense the contrast between rough and smooth, dull and shiny, hard and soft. Observe the changes on certain surfaces that are brought about by weather, light, and color. Weathered wood has a different appearance when it is wet than when it is dry, in the sunlight and in the shade.

Paint that has dried, cracked, and peeled is the kind of texture artists like to capture. This section of paint shows the stress of nature and has patterns of light and shade and interesting shapes.

HOOKED WALL HANGING WITH STITCHERY. Henry Stahmer. Wool, leather, and cotton yarn. Looped and cut wool pile hooked into a canvas backing has rich surface textures.

The texture of weathered wood has an unusual surface quality.

Using Texture

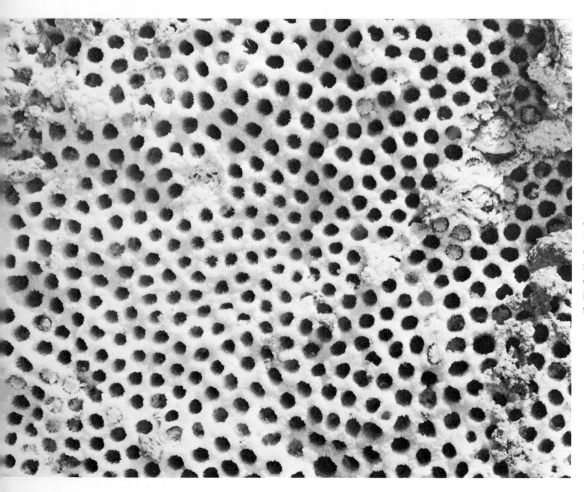

Small objects either enlarged or looked at very closely have a texture and natural design that are often missed by the casual observer. Studying the surface of this piece of coral or any object of nature can inspire marvelous ideas for the artist.

Smooth and scratched surfaces are contrasted in this plaster sculpture.
Student, Institute of Design, Chicago

An eighth grade student fills spaces with visual textures using colored inks and real textures of stones, flock, cellophane, spangles, saw-dust, vermiculite, marble dust, and pencil shavings. *Robert Bonn, Forest Road School, LaGrange Park, Illinois*

Textures are made by impressing textured objects in clay; the objects include a rubber tire, chain, fan, shells, and washers. The clay was cast in plaster for permanence. *Student, Institute of Design, Chicago*

Using Texture

In the illustrations throughout this book notice how artists represent or suggest texture in paintings and sculptures and how they rely on a contrast of textures. There are textures such as silks, satins, velvets, hair, skin, flowers, trees, and wood — both real and suggested by paint. Artists often apply thickly built-up paint to a canvas and scrape and scratch it to achieve texture. Many artists use wool for weaving and fabric for collage and stitchery; then they contrast the textural surfaces of these materials in a composition. Sculptors use the natural textures of wood, metal, and stone to develop works that will please the eye and the sense of touch. It is unfortunate that one may not touch sculptures in museums. Artists are delighted when those who own their works enjoy handling or running their fingers across the carefully developed surfaces of the materials.

MACRAMÉ FORM. (Detail.) Roger Thomason. Goat hair yarn, mohair, and duck feathers contrast with the smooth surfaces of the cowrie shells.
Collection: Phoebe Mooney, Kansas City

ANCESTRAL HEROES. African Sculpture. Primitive artists capture textures in wood sculptures by gouging and painting the surfaces.
Courtesy: Vincent Price Gallery, Chicago

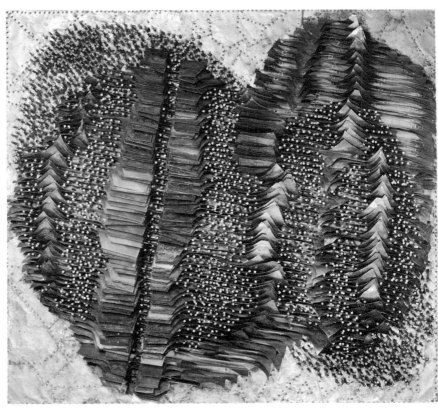

PETIT SOIR LE MATIN.
Zoltan Kemeny. 1959. Using
aluminum and brass, which
have a rich texture of their
own, the sculptor combines
them in such a way that a
a greater surface texture is
achieved by the protruding
shapes and nail heads.
*Courtesy: The Art Institute of
Chicago*

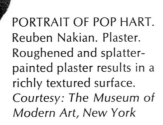

PORTRAIT OF POP HART.
Reuben Nakian. Plaster.
Roughened and splatter-
painted plaster results in a
richly textured surface.
*Courtesy: The Museum of
Modern Art, New York*

83

Using Texture

Try to compose a painting or sculpture with texture by gluing different kinds of string, glitter, broken pieces of noodles, pebbles, and paper onto a piece of cardboard. You can work with many kinds of textured papers and fabrics for a collage. Let your imagination go and see what you can create by using different textures.

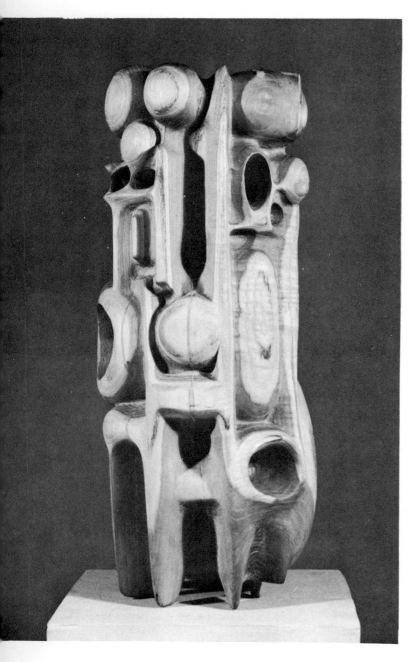

CONVOLUTION. Mychajlo R. Urban. 1966. Locust wood that has been smoothed to a highly polished surface suggests a warmer, more inviting-to-the-touch texture than that of cold metal. *Photo: W. Kacurovsky*

THE DANCER. Paul Klee. 1940. Texture and flat surfa are suggested by combinir small areas of different colored paints and by vary the thickness of the pigmen *Courtesy: The Art Institute Chicago*

HANGING TREE. Donald Seiden. 1969. Bronze and brass are developed with a highly textured, organic surface. The metal could be compared to the kind of texture one sees in the barnacles along a sea wall. *Courtesy: Artist*

NEPTUNE. Alexander Liberman. The smoothness of aluminum suggests a hard, cold, polished surface. *Courtesy: Betty Parsons Gallery, New York*

9

Working with Pattern

A close-up view of protruding bricks reveals a pattern in the brick work and also in the shadows they create, resulting in an intense overall surface interest.

A finished work of art is often referred to as the artist's *design*; it is composed of all the elements discussed so far: line, shape, form, space, color, and texture. In addition, the artist may use any or all of these elements to create a repetition, a movement or accent within his design. This repetitive movement subtly guides the pictorial structure, creates an orderliness that is referred to as *pattern*.

As with many elements of art, we acknowledge pattern but may not take the time to define, observe, or isolate it from other elements of art. We are aware that fabrics in our clothes have a pattern, wallpapers have pattern, patterns are painted on our dishes and pottery. The manner in which veins grow in a leaf creates a pattern. The malfunctioning of a television screen screams with a pattern of jagged lines.

MARINA CITY. Architect,
Bertrand Goldberg. Elements
of artistic observation and
application appear in this
modern complex of buildings.
The complex illustrates
vividly the principle of
repeated pattern in lines,
curves, and enclosed spaces.
*Photo: Bill Engdahl,
Hedrich-Blessing*

Pattern, then, is an additional element of art, and as with other elements, the artist may find his inspiration for pattern in nature and man-made objects. Floral patterns are in clothing and floor coverings; modern buildings exhibit repeated use of lines, shapes, and spaces, thereby employing pattern in a grand scale. How would a building look and function if its windows were placed in a helter-skelter fashion? Our streets are organized in a pattern in order to make our movement around the city more efficient. Architect, city planner, and engineer as well as artist, sculptor, and weaver are all attuned to the importance of pattern in art and our ability to relate to it.

THE GLASS BLOWER. Misch Cohen. Wood engraving. The artist subtly uses repeat patterns in many of his compositions by using the curving thick line and spacing. The circles and ovals also are patterns within the total design.
Courtesy: The Art Institute of Chicago

APPLIQUÉ. (Detail.) Pearron. Pattern is suggested though not exactly repeated in this detail from a fabric wall hanging.
Courtesy: Ontario East Gallery, Chicago

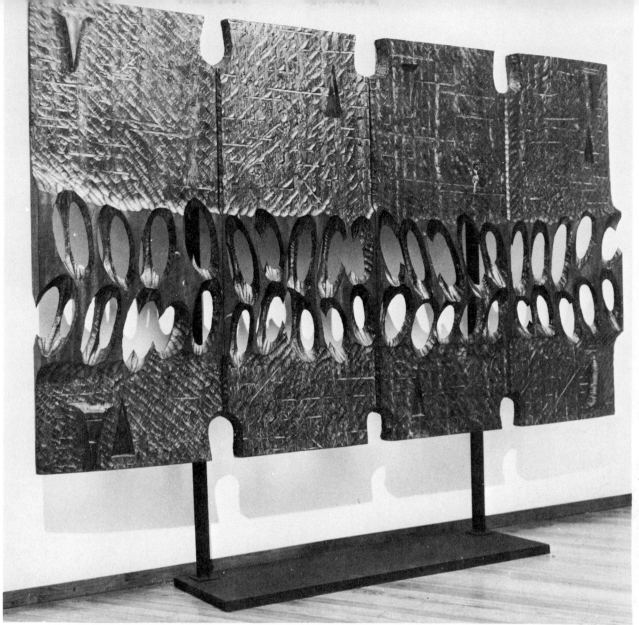

WOOD SCULPTURE.
Tomonori Toyofuku.
Rectangles and ovals create a
pattern.
*Courtesy: Galleria D'Arte Del
Naviglio, Milan, Italy*

The bark of a palm tree is an
example of a natural pattern.
In addition to the repeated
shapes that create the
negative rectangles among
the bark formation, one can
also observe shapes, texture,
and line.

10

Selecting Subjects

JOHN D. ROCKEFELLER.
Alexander Calder. Wire.
Courtesy: The Art Institute of Chicago

Each chapter of this book has emphasized one of the elements of art. A quick review will also illustrate that each work of art has a subject. A walk through a museum will reveal that practically everything in the world has at some time and in some manner inspired artists. Country landscapes and city streets, seascapes, buildings — from magnificent cathedrals to shabby huts — sporting events and entertainment, parades, weather conditions, flowers, food, animals, people at work and play, and countless other subjects appear on canvas, as sculpture, or in other media. In addition, artists, like writers, tell stories. They preach sermons and morals, voice opinions about politics, indicate their religious feelings, cry out against war and poverty, and express their personal fantasies.

WOMAN BEFORE AN
AQUARIUM. Henri Matisse.
1921. Oil on canvas.
*Courtesy: The Art Institute of
Chicago*

THE TRIAL. Jack Levine. 1953-
1954. Oil on canvas. The
artist captures a real event
and gives it a satirical twist.
*Courtesy: The Art Institute of
Chicago*

Selecting Subjects

People who look at a painting and instantly decide whether or not they like it often miss much of the message the artist intended to convey. Art must be considered not only by its elements but also by its subject. Subjects have different shades of meaning, depending upon the artist's background and the period in which the work was created. Therefore, we must not hastily dismiss, for example, a realistic religious painting done in the fifteenth century because it isn't relevant to modern thinking.

BODHISATTVA ON A PEDESTAL. T'ang Dynasty. A.D. 618-906. Sculptors in India and China concentrated on portrayals of religious figures. Subjects were not people; features and shapes for these figures were dictated by a set of rules, or "canons," designed to evoke a divine and superhuman being.
Courtesy: The Art Institute of Chicago

EMPRESS THEODORA AND HER ATTENDANTS. About A.D. 547. Many subjects in this mosaic, from the wall of the church at San Vitale, Ravenna, Italy, are royalty.

MARS AND VENUS UNITED
BY LOVE. Paolo Veronese.
Venetian, 1528-1588. Oil on
canvas. The story of Mars and
Venus is from Roman
mythology.
*Courtesy: The Metropolitan
Museum of Art, Kennedy
Fund, New York*

BETWEEN ROUNDS, NO. 1.
George W. Bellows. 1916.
Lithograph.
*Courtesy: The Art Institute of
Chicago*

A painting should be viewed as representing the age and character of the time in which it was painted and the artist's thinking and abilities at that point in history. For this reason we constantly study history to learn about the changes that man has evolved, not only in art but in other aspects such as science, mathematics, astronomy, and anthropology. The art of the world often tells more about man's history than most other things he has left behind. Through art we see how people lived, how they dressed and decorated their homes, how they constructed buildings, and how they traveled, worked, played, and socialized.

THE EPIPHANY. Giotto. Florence, Italy. Before 1337. Tempera on wood. The artist tells a story about religion and illustrates an event with emotional significance. *Courtesy: The Metropolitan Museum of Art, Kennedy Fund, New York*

STILL LIFE. Peter Claesz. Dutch. About 1625. Oil on canvas. Dutch painters delighted in taking their subjects from still life, such as food, linen, lace, silver, and glassware. *Courtesy: The Art Institute of Chicago*

animals in many moods. The tiger, though seeming to rest, nevertheless appears to have all his senses alert for impending danger. Observe the painted texture in the tiger's fur and in the plants, mountains, and sky.
Courtesy: The Art Institute of Chicago

ON THE TERRACE. Pierre Auguste Renoir. 1881. Oil on canvas. Renoir delighted in painting the effect of light and air on flowers, trees, and people.
Courtesy: The Art Institute of Chicago

The artist portrays the world about him in pictures just as the author records it in words. Sometimes he does this so simply and clearly that we can read his message without effort. Other times his images may require insight into his thinking because he uses symbols or is abstract in his presentation. Often the titles of a work will be the necessary clue to interpretation; other times they will not matter.

IMPROVISATION NO. 30. Wassily Kandinsky. 1913. Events of history are shown in an expressionist manner. At lower right, using wild colors and shapes that are not true representations of the objects, the artist shows a cannon exploding. Other images refer to the buildings and devastation of war. *Courtesy: The Art Institute of Chicago*

THE RAPIDITY OF SLEEP.
Yves Tanguey. 1945. Oil on
canvas. A group of painters
portrayed dream sequences
and showed realistic subjects
in unrealistic, dreamlike
settings. Their paintings are
called *surrealistic*.
*Courtesy: The Art Institute of
Chicago*

THE BULLS OF BORDEAUX:
THE DIVIDED RING.
Francisco Goya. 1205.
Lithograph. At first the
subject appears to be only the
bullfight. Closer observation
of the faces of the people
and the facelessness of the
crowd suggests the artist's
reaction to killing for sport.
*Courtesy: The Art Institute of
Chicago*

Art is constantly changing, as is the world and the people who inhabit it. The more we observe works of art in the past and in the present and understand how the artist works, the better we are able to appreciate what the artist tried to tell us in the past and what he is saying today. The best way to approach an understanding of a work of art is with the same senses that the artist has developed in a special way. Only then will you be able to appreciate the mental and creative processes the artist uses to capture the world in art.

THE FAMILY. Marisol. 1962. Painted wood and other materials. Both title and work illustrate the artist's subject. The materials used to make a contemporary statement include wood, paint, real shoes, and old doors, among other things.
Courtesy: The Museum of Modern Art, New York

AT THE MOULIN ROUGE.
Henri de Toulouse-Lautrec.
1892. Oil. People in night-
clubs were favorite subjects
of Toulouse-Lautrec. From
these paintings we can see
how the French people of the
nineteenth century dressed
and spent their leisure time.
*Courtesy: The Art Institute of
Chicago*

Selecting Subjects

PALETTE OF KING NARMER
FROM HIERAKONOPOLIS.
B.C. 3200. Slate. Subjects
from early Egyptian history
reveal the king's subjection of
his enemies along with
symbolic images. This is
believed to be the earliest
work of art illustrating a
specific personage and event.
*Courtesy: Egyptian Museum,
Cairo*

SECTION OF WEST WALL
OF TOMB OF UNISANKH.
Early 6th Dynasty. Egyptian.
Sculptors depicted scenes
from the hunt in low relief on
walls of tombs.
*Courtesy: Field Museum of
Natural History, Chicago*

RAINSTORM AT SHONO
PASS. Hiroshige. Woodcut
print. This famous Japanese
printmaker often showed
people's reactions to the
weather.
*Courtesy: The Art Institute of
Chicago*

THE DEATH OF SOCRATES.
Jacques Louis David.
French, 1748-1825. A
historical event is portrayed.
*Courtesy: The Metropolitan
Museum of Art, Wolfe Fund,
New York*

Index

Index

THE DEATH OF SOCRATES.
Jacques Louis David.
French, 1748-1825. A
historical event is portrayed.
*Courtesy: The Metropolitan
Museum of Art, Wolfe Fund,
New York*

RAINSTORM AT SHONO
PASS. Hiroshige. Woodcut
print. This famous Japanese
printmaker often showed
people's reactions to the
weather.
*Courtesy: The Art Institute of
Chicago*